THE CURTAIN RISES

Ladies and gentlemen, please take your seats. The performance is about to begin . . .

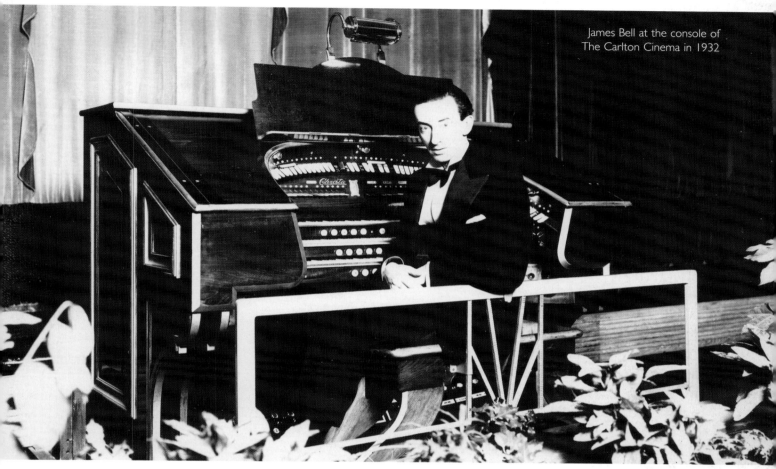

James Bell at the console of
The Carlton Cinema in 1932

THIS is a true story and all the people who feature in it are real. They are YOU.
Any resemblance to actual Liverpudlians and cinemas, living or dead, is totally intentional.
Lights down. Now switch off your mobile phones, keep the noisy,
boiled sweet wrappers quiet – and don't crunch the popcorn too loudly.
Welcome to the flickering screens . . . and the dreams of yesteryear.

THE LOST CINEMAS OF LIVERPOOL

Starring Peter Grant as *Himself*
Director: Colin Hunt
Producer: Vicky Andrews
Special Effects: Zoe Bevan
Stunt Coordinator: Brian Johnston
Runner: Mike McGuinness
Body Double: Colin Harrison
Original Soundtrack: Matthew Barnes
Printed by PCP

Pictures courtesy of Liverpool Daily Post and Echo Archive, Liverpool Records Office
and National Museums Liverpool. Star portraits and film stills from Daily Post and Echo Archive all
copyright of various distributors including Warner Bros, United Artists and Disney.

Produced by Trinity Mirror Media
Best Boy: Mark Dickinson, Gaffer: Ken Rogers
Key Grip: Steve Hanrahan, Script Supervisor: Paul Dove, Cinematographer: Rick Cooke
Trinity Mirror Media Marketing Executive: Claire Brown, Sales and Marketing Manager: Elizabeth Morgan
Sales and Marketing Assistant: Karen Cadman

CONTENTS

Trinity Mirror Media

© Trinity Mirror / Liverpool Daily Post & Echo

ISBN 9 781906 802806

PHANTOM EXPRESS

The foyer of The Trocadero Cinema in Camden Street, off London Road, in 1932.
In 1950 it was taken over and renamed the Gaumont, and closed in 1974. In this picture the
foyer of The Trocadero was decorated as a GWR (Great Western Railway) station to publicise
The Ghost Train, which starred Jack Hulbert – the Arthur Askey version appeared in 1941

A GREAT ESCAPE

Journalist and author Ken Rogers relives the adventures of Saturday morning cinema.

I ALWAYS smile when I watch re-runs of that classic TV war series *Colditz* featuring, the notorious German castle and prisoner-of-war-camp Oflag 1V-C where a band of indefatigable Allied officers continually plotted and planned a series of audacious escapes during the Second World War.

As a youngster, born three years after the end of the hostilities, I always felt we were inspired to reverse the Colditz escape mentality every Saturday morning as we tried to break into the formidable, dark and 'dangerous' environs of our local Liverpool picture houses – intent on sharing in the adventures of the super heroes who inspired us from the big screens.

In Colditz, a searchlight beam would sweep the courtyards and alleyways of the imposing castle, looking to capture any sign of an impending break-out.

In the cinemas of Liverpool, the torches and eagle eyes of the uniformed usherettes would be scouring the darkness for signs of an impending break-in!

The Oflag 1V-C officers would crawl on their stomachs through dank and narrow self-made tunnels to breach the Colditz walls. The kids of the Saturday Matinee would crawl on their stomachs under rows of seats and down dark passageways to reach their goal, the Exit Doors with their push-bar release mechanisms.

Suddenly a shaft of sunlight would pierce the darkness in the corner of the building, and kids would scramble in for a free show, disappearing into the shadows as torch beams flashed across the seats to try and identify the intruders. It was all a game, an integral part of the show. After all, we were all fully paid up members of the 'ABC

LIFE IN THE FAST LANE

The Regal, Norris Green, presents the race-car drama *Such Men Are Dangerous* in 1955. The Regal was built by the Regal Cinema Company and later acquired by Bedford Cinemas

Minors Club' and as such were the future of the cinemas, although movie mania would soon be threatened by the new entertainment wonder, a flickering box in the corner of every living room.

At the beginning of each Saturday morning session, the ABC Minors' Song would be played to the tune of *Blaze Away* by Abe Holzmann (1874 – 1939), with the lyrics presented on the screen with a bouncing red ball above the words to help and inspire the young audience.

We are the boys and girls well known as
Minors of the ABC
And every Saturday all line up
To see the films we like
And shout aloud with glee
We love to laugh and have a sing-song
Just a happy crowd are we
We're all pals together
We're minors of the ABC

Singing the ABC Minors' song was part of growing up for tens of thousands of children. Saturday morning matinees were introduced in 1944 to help combat growing delinquency among children whose home-life had been disrupted by the war.

The Rank Organisation were first in the field in 1944 with a series of films produced especially for children's shows. Merseyside's first ABC Minors' Club opened at the Carlton, Tuebrook, in May 1945.

The early shows had 'Monitors', older children who were supposed to keep the younger more excitable element in order. Although Saturday morning matinees are now remembered with great affection, these press cuttings from the time (below) show that while the children loved them, some of the older generation were less than enthusiastic.

Let's be clear. Going to the flicks to see a Saturday morning kids' matinee was almost as daunting an experience as venturing into the tight confines of one of the caged Boys' Pens at our famous city football grounds, where you took your life in your own hands amidst a screaming, heaving mass of teenage testosterone.

The cinemas, with their mysterious passages and staircases, snatched you off the streets on a bright Mersey Saturday morning and swept you up into the total blackness of a cavernous auditorium where for a couple of hours total anarchy reigned, interspersed by moments of sheer movie magic.

THE NEW AGE OF CINEMA

Wartime legislation was a real revolution for our shooting stars.

GOLDEN OLDIES

Top: Alfred Hitchcock's *Blackmail*, the first all British full-length 'talkie' film, in production at Elstree Studios in 1929
Right: Silent film star Buster Keaton

HIGH NOTE

Westminster Hall on Smith Street in Kirkdale opened as a music hall in April 1887 and was typical of the early cinemas which started life as music halls and progressed to become picture houses, as the movie craze gathered momentum. Ironically a similar pattern was repeated years later as cinemas converted to bingo halls and then supermarkets

SUNDAY opening for cinemas was available during the 1930s, but individual cinemas had to apply to Liverpool Justices for permission to open, and each venue was allowed only two Sundays in any year.

One of the first openings was at the Burlington Cinema in Vauxhall Road in 1932 when *Song of My Heart* was shown. The only proviso was that all the proceeds from that performance had to go to Our Lady's Church in Eldon Street.

As a general rule any cinema opening on their designated Sundays had to pay 20% of their takings to charity, eventually this was reduced to 10%.

Regular Sunday opening in Britain was introduced for the benefit of the armed forces under the wartime Defence Regulations and was implemented in Liverpool in June 1941.

Cinemas remained open on Sundays after the war until 1947 when the government allowed local polls for the electors to decide on Sunday opening.

Liverpool went to the polls on May 20, 1947 and by a majority of 26,901 among the 120,978 votes which were cast the proposal was passed.

In October of the same year Liverpool's Theatres and Entertainments Committee authorised the permanent opening of cinemas on a Sunday.

Most circuit-release cinemas played revival double-bills on Sundays rather than new films.

> "One of the first Sunday openings was at the Burlington Cinema in 1932 – the only proviso was that all proceeds went to Our Lady's Church"

New releases were shown Monday to Saturday for six days at cinemas which were part of larger chains.

These films would subsequently be played by other cinemas without access to a circuit release as 'second runs', 'third runs', etc. often taking a year or more to complete their initial round.

MONSTER SMASH

With the emergence of the American horror film in the early 1930s, the British Board of Film Classification – who had already established the U and A classifications in 1912 – introduced a third classification in 1932. The H, applied to "Films which are likely to frighten or horrify children under the age of 16 years", was at this stage advisory and not a formal certificate. H stood for 'Horrific' and 55 films received the rating, the first being Carl Theodore Dreyer's eerie *Vampyr*. Following pressure from local authorities an official H certificate was introduced in late 1937 – the first 'adults only' certificate. The H certificate lasted until 1951, when it was absorbed into the new X certificate. This indicated a film suitable for those aged 16 and over. In 1970, this increased to 18 and over, and in 1982 it was replaced by the 18 certificate.

DIZZY HEIGHTS

Famous for his silent comedies, Harold Lloyd performed many of his dangerous stunts himself, seen here in the historic 'human fly' sequence from the 1923 comedy *Safety Last*

"The cinemas snatched you off the streets and into the blackness of a cavernous auditorium"

CUTTING EDGE

Above: The Bedford Hall Cinema is generally believed to be Liverpool's first purpose built cinema – it was opened on Boxing Day 1910. This accolade is also claimed by the Kensington Picturedrome which obtained its Cinematograph License at the same time. The Bedford was the brainchild of cinema pioneer and independent exhibitor John Wood. It finally closed in 1959 and the building was demolished in 2008. John Wood went on to develop a chain of cinemas, The Bedford Cinema Group. The most notable was the Abbey, Wavertree, which was at the forefront of cinema technology with stereoscopic sound, cinemascope and 3D on the Abbey's giant screen

WORLD OF WONDER

The Atlas, Rice Lane, in 1958 – the year it closed

REWIND TO A GOLDEN ERA

Bill Kenwright, West End producer and chairman of Everton Football Club, recalls a time when the cinemas were front page news.

MY Liverpool is geographically divided by where all the city's cinemas used to be.

I knew every cinema in Liverpool when I was a kid. I was an addict. In those days you would open up the old broadsheet ECHO and see two full pages of classified ads because there were so many cinemas. I went to the pictures every Saturday night with my gran (Lil Jones), who lived at 31 Vallance Road in Anfield.

I drive up every other week with my best mate, Laurie Mansfield, who manages Andrew Lloyd Webber and Tommy Steele, and he now knows my Liverpool off by heart. Whatever route I take, I point out the locations of all the old Liverpool cinemas . . .

GLORY DAYS
Above, the Grand Cinema on Smithdown Road in 1959. Below, inside the Carlton on Moss Lane, Orrell Park, 1930

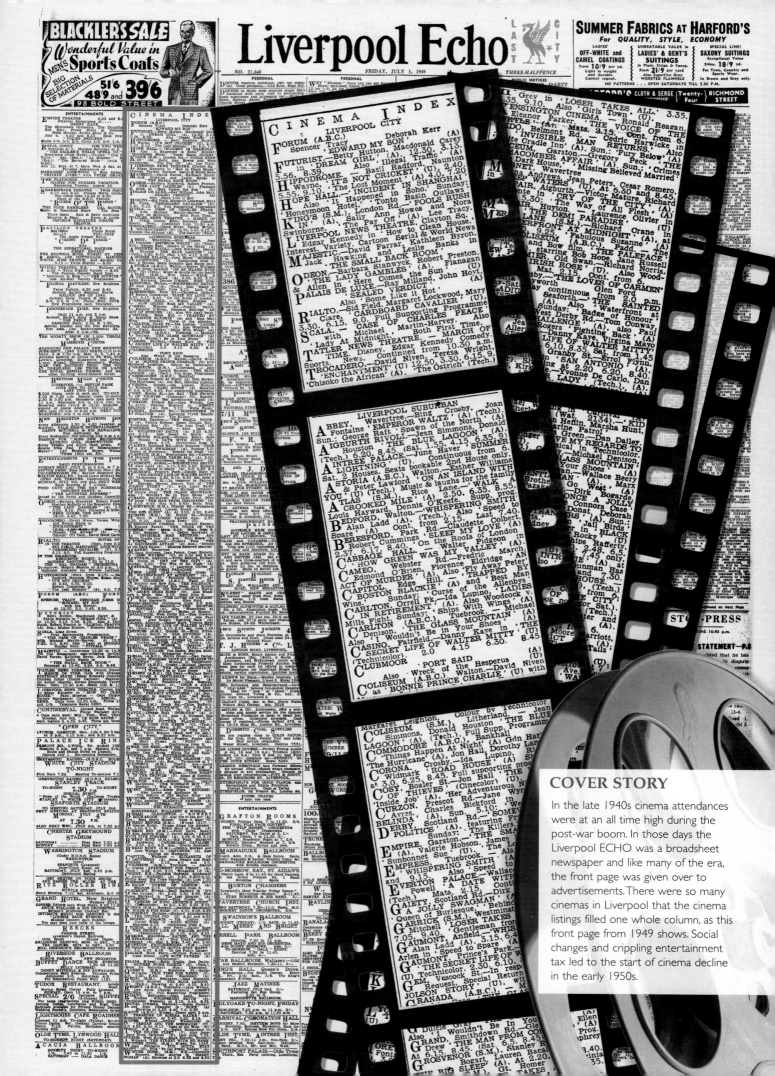

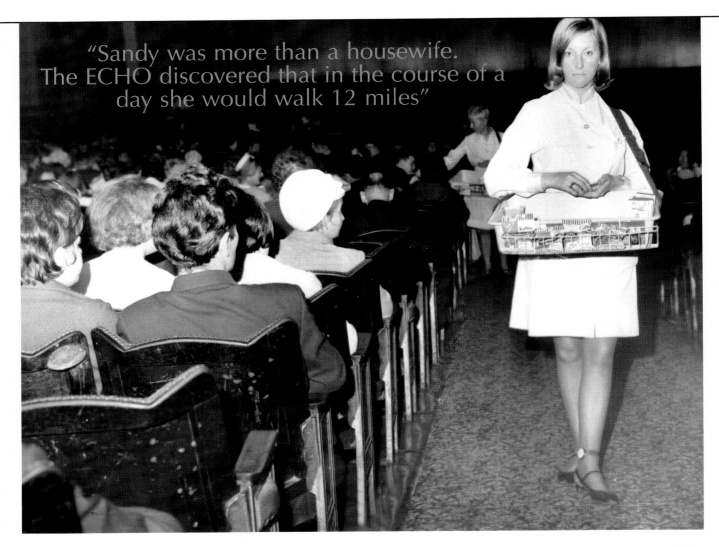

"Sandy was more than a housewife. The ECHO discovered that in the course of a day she would walk 12 miles"

ROLL OUT THE RED CARPET

Cinema played a great part in everyday life in Liverpool and the men and women behind the scenes in our picturehouses were much more than just extras.

THE things they did for love. Back in 1967 the Liverpool ECHO decided it would launch a story with epic proportions.

The newspaper discovered that in the course of a working day in one of the city's cinemas, Liverpool girl Sandy Roberts would walk nearly 12 miles.

25-year-old Sandy, of Everton, was the subject of the ECHO's light-hearted investigation into how far people actually walked. Apart from her 24/7 role as a housewife, looking after her husband and son, Sandy had another job as an usherette at the Odeon Cinema, London Road. Seven nights a week, 6pm until 11pm, with a day off . . . every three weeks.

The ECHO (with Sandy's agreement!) strapped a pedometer to her feet at 6.30pm. For the next half hour people flocked into the Odeon by the score.

At 7pm the pedometer read almost two miles. Between 7 and 8pm the deluge dwindled to a fair-sized stream. And she was able to relax a little – adding another two miles at half the pace.

Then it was time for the beginning of the last programme. Between 8pm and 8.30pm the rush began once more adding a further two miles.

Her score was now six. The last showing of the main feature started at 8.50pm and so the climax of the evening was reached around that point.

Between 8.30pm and 9pm she walked two and a half miles. No sooner had she found one person a seat, it seemed that a dozen others had gathered blindly about the light of her torch.

With the pedometer at eight and a half miles she flopped into a chair in the staff room for a well earned rest and cuppa.

But thirty minutes later she was back on her feet adding another mile before 10pm, just by walking up and down the aisles to make sure everything was in order.

Then it was time to clean the staff room which meant doing the dishes, sweeping the floor and wiping down the tables – another mile.

Three quarters of an hour later the crowds had finally disappeared and the show was over.

But for Sandy and her colleagues there remained one chore to be done – they had to march up and down the cinema in search of any coats or umbrellas that patrons might have left behind.

At 11pm she finally stood outside the darkened Odeon and looked at the pedometer.

It read 11 and a half miles.

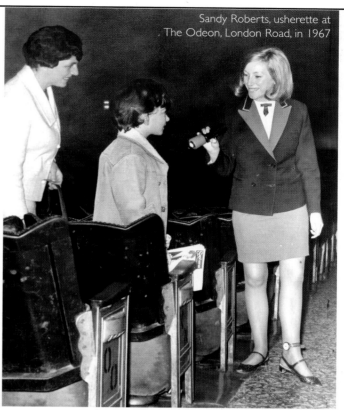

Sandy Roberts, usherette at The Odeon, London Road, in 1967

The ECHO was astonished at this amazing typical usherette of one of our cinemas.

So, typically, the newspaper editorial team asked her to wear it again. The sequel.

This time she wore it from 6pm to 11pm – half an hour longer – and it clocked up 13 miles.

It would have made a great movie one day.

LIVERSPOOL

"We were both howling and rolling around in our seats"

Roger Lyon, Broadcaster

MY mum was dating John, who later became my stepfather.

It was 1964 and we went to see It's A Mad Mad Mad Mad World on the giant screen of The Abbey Cinerama. The cinema was packed, and as a nine-year-old lad, the slapstick humour in the film certainly appealed to me. I thought it was hilarious, an opinion that sadly wasn't shared by John. My mother and I have always had the effect of setting each other off as far as laughter is concerned, and this was a prime example. Very soon, we were both howling and rolling around in our seats, a situation that lasted pretty much the whole length of the movie. John was visibly sinking lower and lower in his seat with acute embarrassment and by the end of the film, it was clear that he was not amused.

Thankfully, the courtship survived this experience and in 1965 they married and celebrated a Ruby Anniversary before John passed away in 2005.

I always make a point of watching that film whenever it is on telly and it will always remind me of that night at The Abbey.

LICENCE TO THRILL

Men of letters, that was Bob Buckles and Brian Sefton, who always had their names up in lights. The dynamic duo braved all weather to tell the great Liverpool public what was on in the flicks.

"People often wonder when we change them," said Bob at the Cannon back in 1988. "They didn't get there by magic. It's a slick operation at least once a week when a new film arrives."

Bob and Dave laughed when they were once asked if they got up at the crack of dawn to do it, as no one ever saw them . . .

BRIEF ENCOUNTER

"Excuse me, Sir, but what is 'Cah Dek?'
"Is it a new foreign film?"

So said this cinema-loving fan, waiting for curtain up on the last night at the Liverpool Palladium in 1967. Mr Geoffrey Manders, manager of the venue, ignored the paparazzi and said: "Look, Mabel, I know you have been a patron here since you were a child but jokes like that won't get you a free ticket on the last night."

Mrs Mabel Howley, of Goldsmith Street, Anfield, howled laughing, and said: "I will miss this wonderful picture palace, young man."

PULLING OUT ALL THE STOPS

David Nicholas has cinema in his blood. This very popular organist has been in attendance at the Philharmonic Hall for more than 20 years making him the longest serving resident organist in the history of the venue. He is a sparkling part of their Classic Movie screening, magically warming up the audience with every feature.

Dave was born opposite the Plaza cinema in Birkenhead and, from an early age, gained a reputation for playing the organ. His first memories of being interested in organ music were the recording that the late Ken Griffin made for Columbia featuring the Hammond organ. Dave was the organ and piano demonstrator at Rushworth's store in Liverpool for two decades. He says: "The Philharmonic organ is a Rushworth classical pipe organ and it did pose a bit of a challenge at first. But audiences have fallen in love with it when this great machine rises majestically from the floor."

But Dave has some regrets. "I never see the last ten minutes of all my favourite films."

He is proud however that he has never missed a night of the Classic Movie shows in 20 years.

THE DARK SIDE

It was a reel change of direction for the city's Royal Court Theatre in 1972, when it reverted to a cinema for the first time in its history, instead of closing for the summer. Going dark as they call it. Pictured is Mr Kerr McKurk in the newly-constructed projection box. And what was the first performance on May 29, 1972? Walt Disney's *Fantasia*.

JOURNEY FOR THE SENSES

Colin McKeown, acclaimed scriptwriter and producer, shares a religious experience.

GIVEN I was from a family of 13 in Huyton, everything to do with life seemed to be small and confined.

I was first taken to join a load of other kids when I was about six-years-old and became an ABC minor.

The ABC minors were like a film club and they did a lot of communal shouting at the screen when baddies came on and lot of cheering when goodies were on! It was my first experience of enjoyment on a grand scale that was synchronised.

I can remember throwing popcorn at the screen from the safety of our seats in the cinema, when a black-hatted villain twisted his moustache and snarled at the camera. We were the righteous, we were the good, we were the brave, we were the white hats, and I always left the cinema with a warm feeling that I had been part of a team that had done good.

The first film I saw was *The Ten Commandments*. Charlton Heston played Moses and when he parted

> "When Moses parted the Red Sea we all jumped back in our seats expecting the ocean to come in on us"

The Red Sea we all jumped back in our seats expecting the ocean to come in on us. It was a very special film because it was a family film.

From that moment Charlton Heston was to me, and a whole generation of kids the same age, a real life Moses, because the size of the screen was so vast and the visuals and effects so real it was impossible to think of the film as fiction.

Being an inquisitive little boy, when they got to the part of Sodom and Gomorrah I asked my Dad to explain where that was and he said he'd tell me after the movie. Funny enough, he never did.

Going to the flicks in the late 50s and early 60s was a sociological phenomenon to see vast arrays of velvet curtain and seemingly acres of marble inlaid with beautiful articulate design. They were like auditoriums of great opulence, they seemed to belong to a past era, one of wealth and posterity. Although they were designed to encapsulate the visual medium they also housed a whole gamut of smells – hot dogs, popcorn, toffee – along with textures, the touch of velvet, the coldness of ice-cream, soap perfume. Your Mum always washed

Charlton Heston in
The Ten Commandments (1956)

your hair to go to the cinema. Then there were colours, vast sweeping arrays of reds and golds, the mammoth silver screen, the flamboyant uniforms of the usherettes and ticket collectors.

They were awesome spectacles designed as compelling oases springing from the grey drabness of the housing estates that surrounded them.

Yes, it was a real treat to go to the cinema and something we all craved for.

What I have come to understand, by taking my young son Zacharay to the cinema, is that when I was his age we all thought that we were stepping into a building that was time locked, a building that was from the past, which would have been home in the Roman era.

The reality is that, I was then – like now – actually stepping into the future because my son's enjoyment and laughter, his emotions of being happy and sad and frightened and exhilarated, are the very emotions I shared at the cinema half a century ago.

I have absolutely no doubt future generations over the next half a century will discover exactly those very same emotions and experiences.

NIGHT ON THE TILES

The Mayfair on Aigburth Road was a grand South Liverpool cinema built on great expectations – a place where you could step through the doors, and escape for a few hours. These pictures were taken in 1937 – the property is now a Home Bargains store

Inside The Mayfair Cinema on
Aigburth Road in 1937

LIVERSPOOL

"Cinema unlocks doors"

Eithne Browne, Actress
I FIRST saw Bambi and I cried.

Then it was a world of fantasy and imagination for me. Cinema unlocks doors. Makes you think.

I later went to see Calamity Jane at the Abbey Cinerama and I danced down the great stairs.

Years later I went to see 2001 A Space Odyssey and I smuggled in my dog, Sarah, under a blanket. I didn't have a footballing boyfriend, but I was obviously a wag then.

I later took my son, Neil, to see Superman. All great memories, but what will always remain in my mind is Fantasia – Walt Disney giving us classical music, and cartoon characters like candles walking up stairs. Fantasia unleashed a world of fantasy on me that I haven't lost and know I never will.

"You know how to whistle don't you Steve? You just put your lips together and . . . blow"

HERE'S LOOKING AT YOU

Screen sirens have raised the temperatures of cinema-goers over the years, but the blonde bombshells of the Fifties, Sixties and Seventies didn't quite match up to their sultry predecessors.

PILLOW TALK

Top: Lauren Bacall has Bogey's Philip Marlowe tied up in knots in *The Big Sleep*. The famous quote is from another Bogart and Bacall classic, *To Have and Have Not*
Right: Nobody could smoulder like Jane Russell, as she demonstrates in her 1956 film *Hot Blood*

LOVELY RITA

Rita Hayworth gets Glenn Ford hot and bothered in the tale of their doomed love affair, *The Loves of Carmen*, made in 1948

COVER GIRL

The Girl Can't Help It was intended to be a vehicle for All-American sex symbol Jayne Mansfield in 1956. Ironically the standout moments were all about the music which made the movie one of the best rock 'n' roll films ever made

MIGHTY MAJ

PETE McGOVERN was a legendary poet, singer song-writer who captured the atmosphere of by-gone days. He wrote the classic In My Liverpool Home, and could turn his hand to most themes, as he did with this tale of entertainment in (and outside) the cinema.

THE MAJESTIC

I wandered around Liverpool just the other day
And the memories flooded back the way they do
There used to be a chippy there and there stood my old school.
And there: stood the Majestic and its queue
The Majestic was a cinema, we all called it the Maj
And the pictures weren't continuous, like today
So once you'd missed the first house
You queued along the wall
And the buskers would arrive and start to play
A one-legged guitar player, a clog dancer from Wigan
A fellow who whistled standing on his hands
But my favourite was the man who played the zither
I'm sure the strings he used were 'lazzie bands'.
He was scared stiff of policemen, so when he played a tune
He wheeled the zither, on its pram, up to the queue
He was after a collection, but we'd all begin to shout
"Paddy Kelly, Paddy Kelly's after you!"
Paddy Kelly meant policeman in the slang we used those days
So the frightened little man, took to his heels
I can see him clear as daylight, him, the zither, and the pram
And hear the terrified squeaking of its wheels
We were thoughtless I suppose, young people often are
Just a joke, a leg-pull, make him look a fool
The poor old bugger could be starving but little did we care
Hard times make harder people as a rule
Now the 'Maj' has been knocked down,
And so has half the town.
The buskers play in sub-ways underground
I always give them money,
guilty conscience,
I suppose.
Perhaps it dims the pram
wheels' squeaking
sounds.

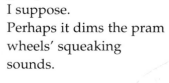

Inside The Majestic on
Daulby Street,
Liverpool city centre

A SPACE ODYSSEY

Journalist and author Ken Rogers recalls how the adventures of our screen heroes were a recipe for a cauldron of excitement and action, on and off the screen.

MY cinema super hero was Flash Gordon, matched only by my comic hero Dan Dare. I had Dan Dare wallpaper adorning the bedroom walls in our Everton terraced house and every night I played out a sci-fi adventure alongside Dan, defending Planet Earth from The Mekon, the super-intelligent ruler of the Treens.

This would take on a whole new meaning every Saturday morning when I visited either the Popular Cinema (The Pop) on Netherfield Road North or the Astoria on Walton Road where Flash Gordon had his regular big screen battles with Emperor Ming The Merciless.

Kids were captivated by these outer space adventures which unfolded week by week, always leaving us with a terrifying cliff-hanger.

My father worked in a number of Liverpool cinemas and so I was able to go behind the scenes and witness the technicalities of the projection room.

I always found cinemas to be ghostly places once their audiences had disappeared into the night, leaving the buildings strangely silent and empty while minutes earlier the sights and sounds of the movie adventures had been absolutely spell-binding.

When they eventually closed down 'The Pop' in the late 1950s, I can remember being one of an army of young local boys who could not wait to get into the empty and now derelict building, marauding up and down the old staircases and passageways and even climbing high up into the roof space.

I recall that two tramline joists had been exposed, stretching from the back of the cinema at roof level

BEHIND THE SCENES

The projection room of The Futurist Cinema, Lime Street, in 1938

MORNING GLORY

Not the sort of bill the young Ken Rogers would have seen at the Astoria on Walton Road

Buster Crabbe as the intergalactic hero Flash Gordon

to a position high above what had previously been the big screen, probably 30 or 40 feet in the air. With a knee on each of these joists, I edged forward to traverse above my former flicks domain. All the kids were daring each other to do it.

Those joists could have been rotten and we could have all plunged into the first row of the pit, but we did it in the name of Flash, Hopalong Cassidy, Roy Rogers and the rest. Of course, many of the old cinemas could also be very basic and, in researching my book *The Lost Tribe of Everton and Scottie Road* I found out that in the dark days of the Depression in the 1930s, it wasn't just money that gained you entry into Liverpool cinemas.

My own father recalls going to the old picture house in Everton Road and gaining entry by handing over a couple of jam jars, something confirmed to me by Terry Cooke, a fellow local author. Terry told me: "There were two cinemas in our area, one the respectable Roscommon where they had a doorman who demanded you had cash.

"Then there was the Tivoli with its wooden seats. It was a deplorable place, but loved by many. They would let you in for three or four jam jars."

The modern multiplexes somehow don't cut it for me. It's like watching a film in your living room.

A visit to the cinema from the Thirties to the Sixties was not just about the films, but rather an exciting, amazing experience, often in an art deco environment of true glamour. Sadly, we will never again see the likes of those spectacular picture palaces of the past.

DECADES OF DREAMS

Going to the cinema wasn't just about the fantastic, epic films that captured our imagination, it was about the whole experience, equal to that of going to some of the great theatres.

THE cinema builders created picture palaces that oozed with magic because of the sheer luxury and the décor.

Some of the souvenir programmes highlighted on this page sum up the whole mood of going to the pictures in the Fifties and Sixties.

These publications were produced to support massive blockbusters like *Ben Hur*, *Ryan's Daughter*, *How The West Was Won* and *My Fair Lady*.

A programme was not made available for every movie. However, some of the really classic film productions clearly justified high quality printed souvenir programmes which became collectors' items in their own right. They featured information on the production staff as well as the stars and gave an insight into how the films were made.

Many of the major films at this time were over three hours long and this inspired the practice of having a very civilized formal intermission during which cinema goers could have refreshments and discuss the quality of the performance before returning to see the final part.

Many of the cinemas were classic Art Deco with fantastic lighting and fittings, which added to the sense of luxury and occasion for everyone who attended. The staff of course, would be superbly turned out in special uniforms.

It is little wonder that cinema goers felt special themselves. Liverpool had its share of specialist picture houses.

The Tatler in Church Street majored on cartoons and was a magnet for kids from all over the city.

The News Theatre on Clayton Square showed short and highly stylized news reels from the world famous Pathe News stable.

These were the days, of course, before 24 hour news on the TV.

People would be able to see footage of events like the Grand National or the FA Cup Final for the first time on any sort of screen.

The power of the cinema was highlighted by the fact that the Liverpool ECHO front page, rather than being totally news-driven, was dominated by advertising, mainly featuring local cinemas.

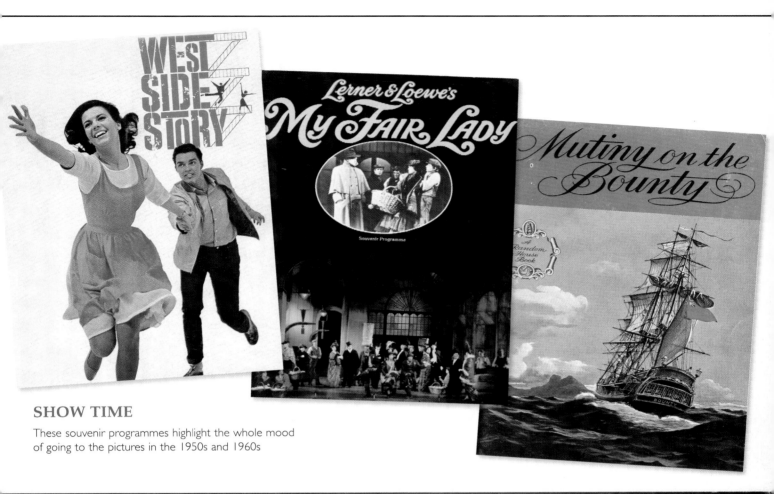

SHOW TIME

These souvenir programmes highlight the whole mood
of going to the pictures in the 1950s and 1960s

ODEON'S STARRING ROLE

Give My Regards to London Road ...

THE ODEON in London Road was one of the great picture palaces of Liverpool and has its place in the city's musical heritage.

It has since moved to Liverpool ONE, but the original venue hosted the likes of Bill Haley and His Comets in 1957. The building is mentioned by guides on daily Beatle fan tours to this day.

On October 7, 1963 it was the venue for two performances by The Beatles following a buzzing Beatlemania afternoon at the nearby Empire Theatre.

On July 10, 1964, the same day The Beatles had been honoured at a civic reception at Liverpool Town Hall, the Odeon also became the setting for the Northern Premiere of the first Beatles' film *A Hard Days Night*. Hollywood came to Liverpool at a Scouse-style red carpet event, with crowds the likes of which the cinema had never seen before.

Ten years later, on November 28, 1984, solo Beatle Paul and his wife Linda, then Wings, flew in to attend the UK premiere of his film *Give My Regards to Broad Street*. Again the Liverpool Odeon, under the leadership of legendary manager George Cranfield, became famous across the UK.

And ten years further on, the film *Backbeat* – the story about the Fab Four's early days in Hamburg – was premiered.

The Odeon, London Road, presents the premiere of *Give My Regards to Broad Street* in 1984

MACCA AT THE MOVIES

Paul McCartney and Tracey Ullman in
Give My Regards to Broad Street

LIVERSPOOL

The Force unleashed

Johanne McAndrew, Screenwriter

THE first film I ever saw was when I was just five. My mum took me to the Odeon on London Road to see *The Shaggy D.A.* – it was a 1976 movie about a giant old English sheepdog that roams the earth.

It didn't inspire me to go and be a screen-writer – just gave me a morbid fear of dogs.

Looking back, we only went to see that one film in particular because the queue for *Star Wars*, at the ABC, was about two miles long and me and my mum got a big cob on.

I never saw *Star Wars* until I was 25 – and had to lie all those years and pretend I had.

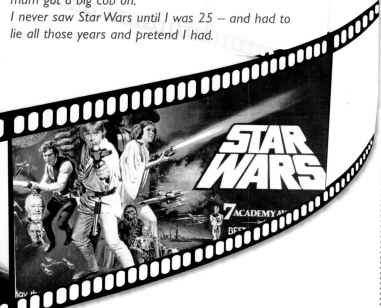

ON CUE FOR HOLLYWOOD

There was something about the movies for George Harrison — he loved the pictures.

GEORGE saw Bill Haley's *Rock Around the Clock* with a certain teddy boy called John Lennon and would often 'sag off' school (play truant – especially from exams) and watch his favourite movies with his pocket money.

He loved Elvis films and Marlon Brando. Anything that had a musical backdrop.

His sister Louise, who lives in America, recalled in the Liverpool ECHO: "He loved the Abbey Cinema which was a few hundred yards away from our own home in Arnold Grove in Wavertree."

George himself talked about his own movie experiences in his biography *I Me Mine* and *The Beatles Anthology*.

He recalled the picture house was central to his Liverpool community. "Arnold Grove was a bit like *Coronation Street*, though I don't remember

any of the neighbours now. It was behind the Lamb Hotel in Wavertree."

George, a film star himself as a Beatle, later set up Handmade Films responsible for such box office hits as *Mona Lisa*. He also saved Monty Python's *Life of Brian*. In the Oxfordshire home he shared with wife Olivia, in Henley-on-Thames, he would often visit the local cinema, a picture palace he helped save from closure.

TINSELTOWN

Above, George Harrison helped finance films including Madonna's *Shanghai Surprise*. Opposite, The Abbey cinema in Wavertree in 1939

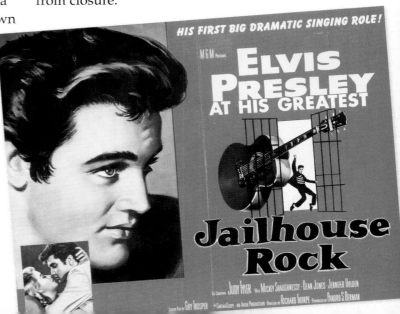

"George loved The Abbey Cinema
which was a few hundred yards away from
our home in Arnold Grove"

LIVERSPOOL

Fangs for the memory

Mike McCartney,
Photographer & Author

I REMEMBER watching films at school with our kid, when we were five or six. The Gaumont in Allerton is a picture house I have great affection for. I saw Christopher Lee in a Dracula film there. Years later, I was on Top of the Pops singing a song called 'Leave It' and I wore a cape. It was given to me by someone who had been at Shepperton Film Studios and it was the same cloak that Christopher Lee had worn.
How's that for a film memory?

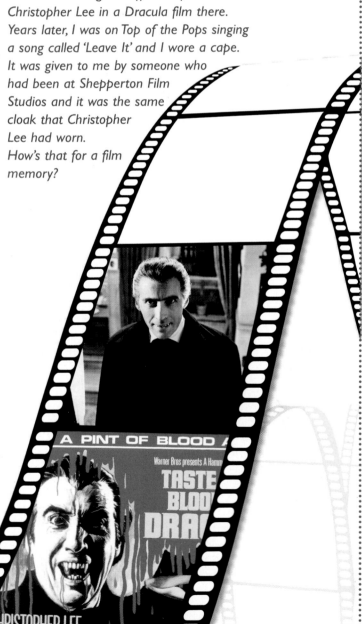

A PINT OF BLOOD

Warner Bros presents A Hamm

TASTE
BLOO
DRA

CHRISTOPHER LEE

Screenplay by JOHN ELDER Produced by AIDA YOUNG
Directed by PETER SASDY Released through WARNER PATHÉ

DIAMOND OF DINGLE

The original Gaumont cinema on Park Road was opened in 1937, on the site of the Dingle Picturedrome, which closed in 1931. In 1966 it became a Top Rank Bingo Club. In its prime from the 1940s onwards, movie-goers included Frankie Vaughan and Gerry Marsden.

The Gaumont on Park Road in 1937

PURE GENIUS

Upper lips didn't come much stiffer than Alec Guinness's Academy Award-winning performance as the unbending Colonel Nicholson in *The Bridge On The River Kwai*

FORCE FAVOURITES

Left: Comedy stars like George Formby kept the spirits up and made sure that the war turned out nice again in films such as *It's In The Air* Right: Noel Coward starred in the 1942 Ministry of Information backed wartime epic, *In Which We Serve*, which was based on the exploits of Lord Mountbatten in command of HMS Kelly when it was sunk in the Battle of Crete

All together now ... Dah, Dah, Dah Dah Dada Dah Dah ... Eric Coates' stirring Dambusters' March has become part of popular culture and was as much a hit as the film, starring Richard Todd as Guy Gibson and Michael Redgrave as Barnes Wallis

KEEPING A STIFF UPPER LIP

Film has always been used for propaganda and putting some backbone into the populace in times of peril. World War II and the aftermath was the golden age for celebrating our British pluck in fighting against the odds.

BRAVE FACE

The everyday work of the British housewife in helping the war effort took centre stage in the 1940 film *They Also Serve*

ON THE EDGE OF OUR SEATS

Johnny Kennedy, tenor and broadcaster, recalls childhood adventures by torchlight.

MY favourite cinema was the Astoria in Walton Road. Not too far away, Brian Epstein was working behind the counter in his dad's shop and he hadn't even heard of The Beatles.

The first film I saw was *Beau Geste* – my dad took me to see it on the Mere Lane. I thought it was fantastic.

Cinemas meant screen idols and there were plenty.

A major male star was John Wayne, an absolute one off and a 24-carat star. I loved Doris Day too – what a voice.

Despite happy days as a kid, in picture houses like The Victory, the Queens, the Everton, the Pop and the Hippodrome . . . I love today's cinemas.

Seats are like armchairs and smoking is not allowed. And the screens are large and clear.

No, I don't long for those old days. In my view, life is so much better now.

My special movie memory is The Astoria and me and my mates went there regularly.

Sometimes we paid and sometimes we bunked in. Being young lads we messed about a bit, cheering during the fights on screen and groaning during the love scenes.

There was no harm in us but we were well known to the guy with the torch. One night, four of us were in and one of the lads put his feet up on the back of the seat in front and the woman sitting in it turned round and told him to put his feet down, which he did. A little later the film ended and the lights came on and the woman in front left the seat to go and buy an ice cream.

As soon as she'd gone, my mate put his feet up again against the back of the seat and to his surprise the back of the seat shot off and we collapsed on the floor with laughter.

Over came the guy with the torch and one minute later we were out in the cold in Walton Road with his words ringing in our ears "You're barred!"

Many years later when I was working for Radio City, the Astoria was no longer a cinema and had been turned into a club.

Radio City booked me in to do the Johnny Kennedy Show with a star-studded line-up which included Micky Finn, Jackie Hamilton and The Hillsiders.

The Astoria was packed and I was really looking forward to appearing on the stage of the cinema where I had spent so many happy hours as a kid.

Suddenly an old chap came up to me with a serious expression his face and said: "You can't go on."

"Why not?" said I.

"Because I barred yer out of 'ere years ago!"

It was the guy with the torch who'd slung us out after the back of the seat shot off.

We had a good laugh about it and I bought him a pint.

But there was one little sting in the tale to come.

I said to him: "Even after you barred us out we still used to come y'know."

He just laughed and said: "I know you did, I used to see you loads of times, but you were only young lads so I didn't bother saying anything."

The on-going magic of cinema days.

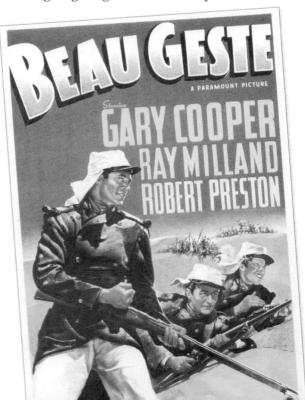

"Being young lads, we messed around a bit, cheering during the fight scenes and groaning during the love scenes"

A FINE ROMANCE

The Astoria on Walton Road in 1930. Right, Doris Day and Rock Hudson embrace in the 1959 film *Pillow Talk*

SATURDAY NIGHT AT THE MOVIES

Who cares what picture you see? The ABC on Lime Street in 1975

SCREEN WITH ENVY

It was a job to die for, writes Peter Grant, former film critic for the Liverpool Daily Post and ECHO.

IT was the best job I ever had. No red carpet – didn't need it, but I enjoyed some of the best premieres in town.

A film reviewer for the Daily Post and ECHO in the early to mid 1980s. You saw films and you didn't pay – you were paid to do this job. Privileged? Yes.

I was a freelance journalist then.

So I was able to go to 'the pictures' at 10am in the morning, because other reporters or features staff couldn't be spared for that amount of time.

Granted it wasn't a great fee. But you sat there and there were no adverts, straight into the movie that would be out the next week, so you could write the review and meet your mates in the pub and tell them you'd seen it first.

You could get lost for three hours in the cinemas from the ABC Lime Street to London Road. Then go into the manager's office at midday and have a drink and some sarnies. Later, relaxed, you could write your review.

> "The cinema was ours for the morning – we could sit where we wanted and we could watch a movie in peace"

And there was just a handful of other writers all like me – radio people; fellow hacks and hackettes; student scribes running their magazines.

But the cinema was ours . . . for the morning.

We could sit where we wanted and we could watch a movie in peace. No kids running up and down aisles (like I used to). I was grown up, and yet, still a kid. No popcorn crunching or boiled sweet munching. It started when they knew we were all in there. Credits rolled. I'll never forget those cinema days. Yeah, I was lucky.

It was the best job in the world and in some of the greatest cinemas in the world. They helped me escape from my own world. Oh, and I miss it.

MOVING IMAGES

By Peter Grant

We stood outside, Dad and me.
He smoked a ciggie . . .
I said what are we waiting for?
Four other brothers,
Stood there too.
"Look, look" said Michael, "we are
going to see *Ben Hur*."
Inside the building everyone smiled,
And I knew something was going on.
A fairground of sorts.
A sweet kiosk. Popcorn.
What's that?
A man in a uniform with a military hat
and gloves opened doors.
Dad led us in like leading a line of ducks
Inside, the biggest telly I'd ever seen.
Nothing happening,
Talk, chatter. Then silence.
As the curtain pulled back,
I was meeting the silver screen for the
first time.
Couldn't wait to get back and tell mam
We went again, and again.
Now I search for the cinemas of my youth
Escapism
Romans
Chariots
Cowboys
Batman
To tell you the truth,
I didn't want to leave.
Dad took us all home,
And we always headed home to the
radio, and looked at the telly.
But inside those childhood places of
dreams
Part of me always remains
The pictures. The pictures.
You know,
After that first visit,
Life would never be the same.

BIBLICAL TALE

Ben Hur and Messala fight it out in the
famous chariot race sequence in *Ben Hur*

Inside The Gaumont,
Park Road in 1937

LIVERSPOOL

Days of our youth

Distant Voices — Still Lives
AWARD-WINNING, Liverpool born Terence
Davies has captured the cinema days of his
youth better than anyone else. His 1988 film
Distant Voices — Still Lives has one memorable
scene where the soundtrack *Love is A Many
Splendored Thing* is played as 50s cinemagoers
sit entranced. The magic of cinemas beautifully
caught on the big screen.

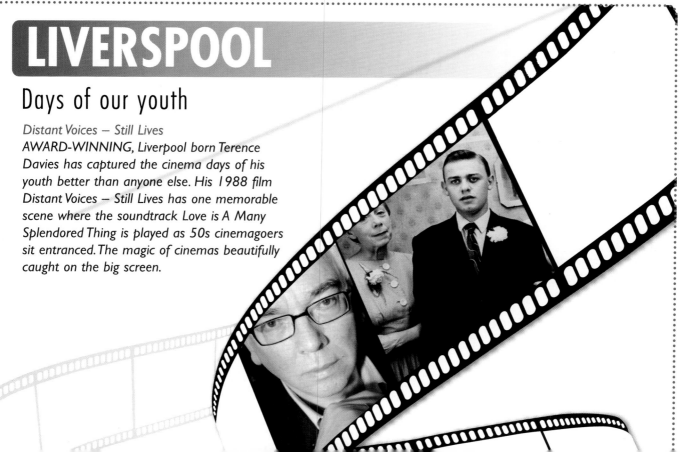

PUTTING ON THE GLITZ

When the Paramount Cinema on London Road opened in 1934 it was one of seven Paramounts built in the UK to provide unparalleled levels of luxury and comfort to the cinema going public.

HIGH SOCIETY

The Paramount cinema cafe was the city's most popular rendezvous, giving many people a small measure of experience of how the other half lived. It was taken over by the Odeon Group in 1942 and renamed shortly afterwards. In 1968 the sumptuous interior was altered to enable the Odeon to become a 2 screen cinema. This was changed again in 1973 to create Odeons 3 and 4. Odeon 5 came along in 1979 and a further two screens were created in 1999. The Odeon finally closed its doors in 2008 to be replaced by a new multiplex in Liverpool ONE and the art deco masterpiece that was the Paramount slipped into the pages of history.

A HAZE OF NOSTALGIA

Local historian Fred O'Brien celebrates the legacy of our cinema pioneers.

IN the 1940s and 50s, probably the high-water mark of British cinema-going, Liverpool film fans had a very wide choice of 'dream palaces' at which to slake their thirst for romance, gangsters, adventure, westerns or whatever took their fancy.

My nearest 'palace' (which wasn't very palatial really) was the Palladium, West Derby Road.

Not far were The Savoy (later a carpet shop), The Lido (we said Lie-doe), The Hippodrome, The Kenny (Kensington), The Majestic (corner of Daulby St), The Carlton Tuebrook, The Lytton and The Cosy.

The last named was small (say 250 seats) but it did have a balcony with a Toblerone mirror on its staircase. The Cosy became a butchery depot. The Kenny became a Worthingtons pub (The Picturedrome, good name).

"Cinema-going wasn't without its hazards. One viewed the screen through plumes of smoke"

The Carlton became a bingo hall, as did many Liverpool cinemas. The Abbey 'defected' to become a supermarket. Before it became a theatre The Everyman had been a cinema.

In 1896 the French cinema pioneers the Lumiere brothers filmed Liverpool street scenes and exhibited the footage at Hope Hall, a gospel hall that occupied the building later to become the Everyman Theatre. A plaque there commemorates this first public cinema screening in Liverpool.

On Lime Street, we had the exotically-named Palais de Luxe, now long-gone. Also on Lime Street is still the forlorn Forum, its ultimate fate is yet to be known. Also still extant is the Futurist, now with its massive illuminated sign exhorting us to THINK ABOUT YOUR FUTURE. Intriguing, but no longer a cinema.

The Woolton opened in 1927 and still survives, just, thanks to Willy Russell and other 'Angels'. Another survivor is the Plaza, Waterloo, kept alive by local community volunteers. Huzzah!

Many other cinemas of fond memory have gone. The Astoria has gone, so have the Lytton, Rio, Trocadero, Commodore, and The Cabbage Hall. (This is not a joke). I saw *Tom Jones* at the Rialto, *Captain from Castille* (Tyrone Power) at the Lido, *Fail Safe* at the Majestic, *Michael Strogoff* at the Palladium, *It's a Wonderful Life* at the Cosy, and *The Searchers* (best film ever made) at The Savoy, Palladium, and Cosy (twice-through each).

Cinema-going wasn't without its hazards. One viewed the screen through plumes of tobacco smoke. At very popular Saturday matinees, an usherette would sometimes come around the auditorium spraying a substance of which little was said. Was it DDT pesticide or perfumed tap water or something else intended to counter the aroma of sweaty young bodies? Today, one can have a virtual cinema of one's own at the touch of a button.

I look back on my (relatively primitive) cinema-going experiences with great affection. I view them now through a pink-tinted haze of nostalgia.

The curtains would swoosh back and I would be transported to wherever that day or night's offering was set. Bliss.

GLAMOUR WHIRL

The exotically-named
Palais De Luxe on
Lime Street in 1959

LIVERSPOOL

"There I was on the screen, 24 feet high"

Louis Emerick, Actor

AN early weekly diet of films made a big impact
on Louis Emerick, because he later became an
actor, not just in Brookside, but on the big screen
in films including Layer Cake.

Louis says the 'flicks' changed his life.

"I used to go to the cinema in Toxteth called The
Granby. My mam would give me pocket money
and me and my mates we would go there on a
Saturday and spend it all and then once we'd
seen the features we would run down Upper
Parliament Street to The Rialto."

And Louis can recall the first BIG film he saw.

"It was A Night To Remember, about the Titanic
and starring Kenneth More.

"I remember when I first appeared in a film and
there I was, 24 feet high, or something like that,
on the big screen. That was the same lad who
used to sit in The Granby and The Rialto all those
years before."

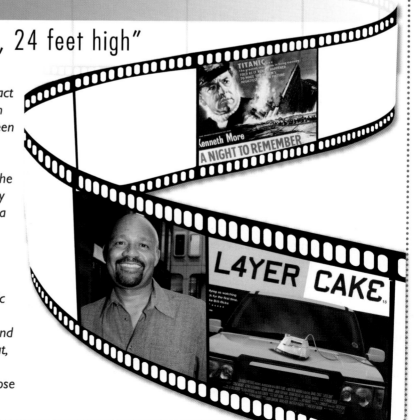

One of Liverpool's great locomotive trains proved a roaring success in film.

IN 1837 the Liverpool and Manchester Railway ordered two locomotives to haul luggage trains, which were later called 'Lion' and 'Tiger'.

They were the first locomotives built by Todd, Kitson and Laird.

In 1859 Lion was sold to the Mersey Docks and Harbour Board and installed as a stationary pumping engine at Princes Dock.

She was rescued by members of the Liverpool Engineering Society, to which body she was presented by the Dock Board in 1928.

After restoration at the Crewe railway works she took part in the centenary celebrations of the Liverpool and Manchester Railway in 1930, pulling a replica train.

During the period prior to the Second World War, Lion stood on a plinth at Lime Street Station but was removed in 1941 and not replaced.

Lion appeared in three films: *Victoria the Great* (1937), *The Lady with the Lamp* (1951) and *The Titfield Thunderbolt* (1952), the latter making her something of a celebrity in view of its popular appeal.

Lion was stored at the Crewe works and was not seen by the public, apart from her film appearances and railway publicity events.

In 1967 she was loaned to Liverpool Museum (as World Museum was then known) by the Liverpool Engineering Society. This was changed to an outright gift in 1970.

STEAMING ON

The Lion locomotive, pictured in the 1952 film *The Titfield Thunderbolt*

The St James Cinema ('The Jamie')
on Park Road, 1962

FLYING TO THE FLEA-PITS

As a kid, going to the pictures to watch science fiction films was the ultimate treat for Bill Harry, Mersey Beat founder and film buff.

I WOULD have gone to the cinema seven nights a week if I could.

My nearest was the St James Cinema, or 'the Jamie' as we called it. The Saturday afternoons always had Johnny MacBrown films and *Three Stooges* shorts, plus serials like the *Purple Rider*.

The kids used to come out slapping their thighs as if they were riding horses! When sitting waiting for the evening show to start, they always played the same music, an Edwardian music hall song *Down at The Old Bull And Bush*.

Sometimes I'd walk all the way to the Dingle to the Park Palace and sit on hard wooden seats in the gods. We used to call it the 'flea pit', the most uncomfortable cinema we'd ever been in. I remember seeing *The Four Feathers* there. Further along was the Beresford where I saw *The Wizard of Oz* and was completely enchanted by it and I also saw *Blood Alley* with John Wayne. I even went as far as Aigburth to see James Dean in *East Of Eden* and a British version of Edgar Allen Poe's *The Tell Tale Heart* – I think the cinema was just called the ABC.

TWEEZE ME
Sci-fi classic *The Incredible Shrinking Man* (1957)

The front page of the Liverpool ECHO was full of literally hundreds of cinemas. The second cinema we mostly visited was the Rialto in Upper Parliament Street. This was a favourite of mine – my Mum loved to go there and see weepies, the Joan Crawford, Susan Hayward films where the usherettes standing at the back would give you tissues when you went in, for the women to use when they cried! One she liked was *Peyton Place*.

I never broke into a cinema for free but at the Rialto I was aware that kids used to get in by climbing through the window in the gents toilet.

> "The kids used to come out of the films slapping their thighs as if they were riding horses!"

Sunday nights had different bills from the week, showing films such as *Cabin In The Sky* and Paul Robeson movies. One of my favourite actors was Tyrone Power and I liked his films such as *Nightmare Alley*, *The Razor's Edge*, *Captain From Castile*, *The Black Swan*, *The Black Rose* and *Son of Fury*.

The ECHO ran competitions tying in with local screenings and I won a set of prints of drawings of the cast of *The Black Rose* – Tyrone Power, Cecile Aubry, Orson Welles and Jack Hawkins. There used to be horror films classified 'H', which you had to be 16 to get in to see.

A boyfriend of my mum's took me to see *The Thing From Another World* at the Futurist, even though I was under age – it was fantastic.

My favourite films were science fiction. I remember queuing up outside the Odeon to see *The Conquest of Space* – and I also saw Charlton Heston at the Odeon – in those days, sometimes famous film stars came to England to promote their films at British cinemas.

I remember seeing *The Man From Planet X* at the Futurist – terrible film, but I loved *The Incredible Shrinking Man*, *Forbidden Planet* (which I saw at the Majestic) and my favourite was *War Of the Worlds*. ➤

CENTRE STAGE
Hope Hall – now The Everyman Theatre – in 1973

➤ Incidentally, Gerry Marsden saw *Carousel* at the Futurist and it encouraged him to include the song *You'll Never Walk Alone* in his repertoire.

Those days I'd see every sci-fi movie, which were popular in the fifties – *Them*, *The Beast From 20,000 Fathoms*, *The Creature From the Black Lagoon*, even turkeys like the British made *Fire Maidens From Outer Space* (which I saw at the Majestic), although Britain did come out with some great sci-fi with the *Quatermass* movies (which I saw at the Forum), which then led Hammer films into their horror cycle. I remember one time, my girlfriend (now wife) Virginia and I were on the top deck of a bus into town and as we entered Cosy Street I saw a cinema there which was showing *The Invasion of the Body Snatchers*. Even though I'd seen it before, I dragged Virginia off the bus and saw it again!

Films used to have promotions. I remember when *Samson & Delilah* was at the Odeon, London Road and they borrowed the huge Samson & Delilah oil painting from the Walker Art Gallery and displayed it on the stairs to the circle.

I also used to go into town. In Lime Street, on one side of the road was the Palais de Luxe and the ABC Forum (when I was at the art college I noticed John would take Cynthia to the Palais, occasionally accompanied by Rod Murray).

Opposite was the Scala and the Futurist. In London Road there was the Odeon and opposite, in Camden Street, the Trocadero, which later became the Gaumont. Further up, past TJ Hughes was another little cinema, it may have been called the Essoldo. I first saw *Invasion of the Body Snatchers* there and also a film called *Liane Jungle Goddess*. It was about a white girl living in the jungle. I imagined it to be a bit like a female Tarzan, but I was surprised when it turned out to be a teenage German girl – who was topless!

Talking of Tarzan films, I used to go to the Hope Hall to see them. And that was the cinema I also saw my first Brigitte Bardot films. Coming out of the Hopey after seeing a Tarzan movie, I'd climb into the trees outside the Liverpool Institute on the Duke Street side.

There were always queues to get into cinemas those days, particularly at weekends and on Sunday nights.

While you were waiting in the queue you were usually entertained by buskers – not the musical kind, but ones who had themselves chained, then stuffed into a canvas bag which they had to get out of – cut price Houdinis! Also popular were copies of *Billy's Weekly Liar*, a paper full of jokes which would be sold to the waiting crowd.

You would often wait in a queue, then you'd be told that only the dear seats were left.

When you made a decision that you'd pay the extra, the crowd would move up and then you'd be told the cinema was full.

So you'd rush to another cinema, but sometimes it was too late and you never got to see a film that night.

"A boyfriend of my mum's took me to see *The Thing From Another World* at the Futurist, even though I was under age – it was fantastic"

BACK TO THE FUTURE

The Futurist on Lime Street in 1938. The final credits rolled at the Futurist on July 1982. Innovations such as Todd-AO, 70mm six-track stereo and Sensurround were unable to stop the inevitable, and the 860-seater cinema closed with the double bill of *Blazing Saddles* and *History of the World Part 1*. It had opened in 1912 as the Lime Street Picture House, then an early purpose built cinema in the city centre. It was also one of the first cinemas in Liverpool to show 'talkies'

The Granada cinema, East Prescot Road, in 1932

LIVERSPOOL

Guitar greats

Les Dennis, Actor

I'M a South Liverpool lad and me and my sister, Marg, loved going to the pictures. I remember seeing The Young Ones starring Cliff Richard and The Shadows. All the way home I looked at my own 'shadow' and I never forgot that moment. I never forgot the experience. Even now, it makes me smile.

WINDOW TO THE WORLD

Ken Dodd, born, raised and still raising a laugh in his beloved Knotty Ash, recalls with great affection, the picture houses of his youth.

THE cinemas of our youth were a window to the world.

There was no telly then – that's how people got their news through the picture houses like the Curzon, the Regent and The Granada in Dovecot.

You didn't have photos taken outside cinemas, there was no point. It was all about what happened inside. Two of my aunties were actually piano accompanists at the cinema.

The pictures also introduced people to comedy greats like Abbott and Costello and Laurel and Hardy. And our very own big-hearted Arthur Askey.

ANOTHER FINE MESS

Left, comedy greats Laurel and Hardy. Above, Ken Dodd with Arthur Askey, who starred in several Gainsborough Pictures films

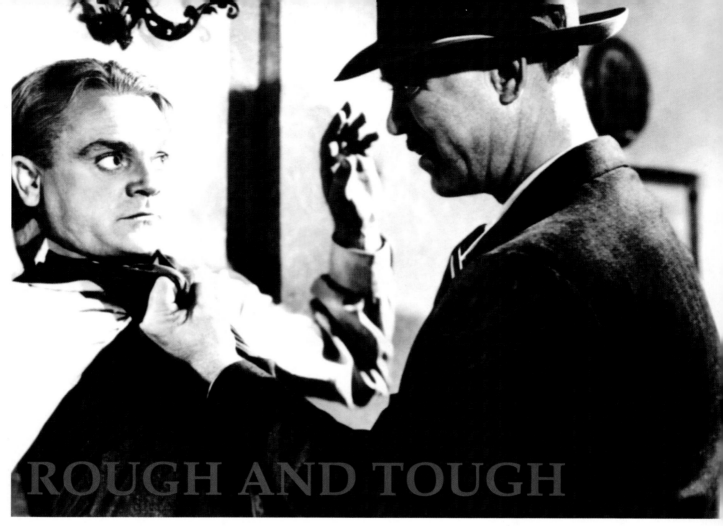

ROUGH AND TOUGH

They were people you simply didn't push around. Cool cats back in the pre-war Forties and Fifties. Hollywood travelled well and influenced young men who would look up to and mirror their idols. On Merseyside, sales of sharp suits and hats soared. Those Yanks had the looks and they had style – charismatic characters played by James Cagney, Robert Mitchum, Humphrey Bogart, Edward G. Robinson and George Raft. In the UK we were later to produce our own anti-heroes such as Albert Finney, as Scouse detective Gumshoe, and, of course, James Bond. Cinema opened up a whole new world – the glamorous macho underworld . . .

FRED MacMURRAY ★ BARBARA STANWYCK
EDWARD G. ROBINSON

From the moment they met it was Murder!

in PARAMOUNT'S

DOUBLE INDEMNITY

PORTER HALL
JEAN HEATHER
BYRON BARR
RICHARD GAINES
JOHN PHILLIBER

MURDER IN MIND

Above: James Cagney and crooked cop Ward Bond in the 1950 gangster thriller *Kiss Tomorrow Goodbye*.
Right: Edward G Robinson, star of *Double Indemnity* (1944)

DRESSED TO KILL

Top, Robert Mitchum and Jack Palance appeared together in *Second Chance* in 1953, notable as the first RKO film produced in 3D. Above, Albert Finney as a private eye in *Gumshoe* — many of the scenes were filmed on location in Liverpool. Right, George Raft starred in several crime melodramas of the 1930s and 1940s

A SOCIAL REVOLUTION

"I was so much older then, I'm younger than that now . . ."
An Old Swan childhood, by Colin Hunt, archivist and author of *Liverpool Then* and *Liverpool Life.*

ABC Minor,
Colin Hunt

IT may have rained in London on Her Majesty's Coronation parade during that momentous day in June 1953, but in Liverpool the sun shone.

As the last jellies at the street party hit the bellies the game was on. Not kings and queens or knights of the realm, but *The Crimson Pirate.*

We brought our screen hero to life with wooden swords and cardboard hats, a much more realistic figure than a remote monarch in London.

Every afternoon that summer we relived the adventures of Captain Vallo, without the style or teeth of Burt Lancaster, but with just as much enthusiasm. The adventures of the screen heroes that we acted out were real life to us.

Saturday mornings meant the ABC Minors at the Regent in Old Swan. Chaos with Pegleg the doorman trying to keep the unruly mob in order.

The usual fare of cartoons, serials and comedy meant the mornings flashed by. There were not just films but various entertainments in the interval.

On one occasion a visit from Peter Farrell the Everton skipper and Billy Liddell from Liverpool led to a "who can cheer the loudest" contest between the fans.

The flickering film breakdowns were regular events causing outbreaks of slow hanclapping and booing, leading to boredom and the speedy descent into mayhem. My favourite serial had to be *Flash Gordon* although the Mud Men that Flash battles in the caves did give me nightmares, I kept seeing them morphing out of my bedroom walls. If only someone would match those early Flash Gordon serials to Queen's mercurial soundtrack to the 1980 film, maybe add a touch of vintage colour, you would have cinema magic.

Apart from Flash Gordon, the highlights were the comedy series, *The Three Stooges* and *The Bowery Boys.* The style of comedy influenced a whole generation of British youth.

Among those influenced were the young Beatles who selected Leo Gorcey and Huntz Hall from the Bowery Boys for the cover of the Sgt Pepper album.

In the end only Huntz Hall appeared, Leo Gorcey had lost his chance of immortality after his agent demanded a $400 fee for the use of his image and he was turned down.

In those days the A certificate meant that a child could be admitted in the company of an adult and often Friday and Saturday evenings were spent hanging round outside the Regent and the Curzon looking for couples (not single men, my mum had decreed) to ask them "take us in please mister".

Hard to imagine anything like that happening today.

The local cinemas were the Regent, Curzon, Swan and New Premier, just a short distance away were the Carlton, Tuebrook and the Granada in Dovecot. The imperative to stick with your own gang on your own turf meant that The Swan and New Premier were off limits.

The New Premier had already been banned by my parents following an outbreak of disorder when Teddy Boys danced to Bill Haley's Rock Around the

"Friday and Saturday evenings were spent hanging around outside the Regent and the Curzon looking for couples, to ask them 'Take us in please, Mister'"

The New Premier Cinema on Prescot Road near Green Lane, 1959

Clock during a screening of the then notorious film *Blackboard Jungle*.

If that film brought rock and roll to life for British youth and started a social revolution, the real breakthrough was *The Girl Can't Help It*.

Intended as a vehicle for the pneumatic Jayne Mansfield, it gave us our first opportunity to see performances by Gene Vincent, Eddie Cochran, Little Richard and the rest. The film gave John Lennon and Paul McCartney their first inspirational view of a generation's rock and roll heroes.

Of all my childhood cinemas none compares with the Curzon in Old Swan.

A magnificent art deco masterpiece with flowing lines that wouldn't be out of place on a south coast hotel in an Agatha Christie novel. The Curzon was ➤

INSPIRATIONAL

The Bowery Boys. Leo Gorcey (second left) missed out on the chance of immortality on the Sgt Pepper cover, unlike Huntz Hall (centre)

➤ designed by Sir Alfred Earnest Shennan, who also designed many other cinemas including the Abbey, Carlton, Plaza, Mayfair and the Forum on Lime Street. In addition to his cinemas he designed The Grafton Rooms, numerous office buildings such as Spinney House and Pearl Assurance House as well as the Grade II* listed Greenbank Synagogue. He also served as city councillor and alderman from 1920 until 1956. He made his mark on every aspect of Liverpool life.

A trip to the Curzon was always an occasion, once inside the marbled halls it felt a world away from our normal everyday lives. This was no "bughouse" or "flea pit". More than most cinemas it was a gateway to another world. Opened in October 1936, this 1750 seater picture palace finally closed in August 1960. The Curzon also hosted wrestling and pop concerts in later years.

With the absence of television in most households many junior schoolchildren in 1953 were, like myself, treated to a cinema double bill of British triumphalism. We queued outside the Curzon in an atmosphere of short-trousered patriotism. First up was *A Queen is Crowned*, a dull documentary of the Coronation narrated by Laurence Olivier, all in glorious Technicolor. ➤

MASTERPIECE

Sir Alfred Earnest Shennan, a man who made his mark on the city. The Curzon's elegant lines reflected in the sumptuous interior. These pictures were taken in 1936

➤ The accompanying feature was a much more superior affair, George Lowe's masterly *Conquest of Everest*. Like the rest of my classmates I sat enchanted by the wonders of nature and the fortitude of man.

The Curzon was one of the few cinemas in the city to show 3D films. *The Charge at Feather River* was reckoned to be one of the finest 3D movies of that period. The shower of spears and flaming arrows shot at the audience had us diving and dodging in our seats.

But the high spot was a rattlesnake's eye view of one of the characters dealing with it by spitting a wad of chewing tobacco in its face. The whole audience lurched backwards in their seats, which was nothing to what happened when a body fell out of a cupboard and into the audience in the 3D trailer for *House of Wax* which followed.

In my teenage years there were standout films that linger in the memory, being scared witless watching *Psycho* at the Carlton, *The Vikings* with its wonderful soundtrack at the Granada, the film being my inspiration for a beard and long hair.

Top of the list was *Jazz on a Summer's Day*, which I saw at the Majestic as many times as I could afford, still the most perfectly constructed music documentary I've seen.

But cinema doesn't stand still and the medium still has the power to enchant and involve, even in its simplest forms.

In 1984 I took my son and an unruly band of ten-year-olds to see *Ghostbusters*. As the lights dimmed and the screen went dark the first bars of Ray Parker Jr's theme tune filled the packed auditorium, there was an explosion of children, and not a few adults, up dancing and singing.

It could have been a Saturday matinee in 1954.

The magic lives on.

A WORLD AWAY

Like an ocean liner moored at the Pier Head the lights of the Curzon twinkle in the darkness, waiting to carry you away to distant lands and magical adventures. Left: *The Vikings* (1958) — a tale of blood and thunder, drunken feasts, axe throwing, amputation, beautiful maidens, fratricide, beards, longboats and long hair, all put to Mario Nascimbene's epic music score

SEE 'EM AND WEEP

Award-winning broadcaster Billy Butler loves 'the pictures' — always has and always will. His six-days-a week afternoon show on BBC Radio Merseyside has won him a lifetime achievement trophy and it was down to the fact that Billy knows his audience and he knows nostalgia inside and out.

A BIG part of his shows centre around the screen idols that he loved. He has interviewed some of the biggest names in the world.

Who else could get Doris Day on a show? Billy Butler could actually go on BBC's Mastermind and answer questions on the whole subject matter of films past, present and future. In Liverpool few people know more about films, lost cinemas, actors, actresses, cinematic icons than Mrs Butler's Eldest.

So what was it about the pictures that can still turn Billy Butler all starry, starry-eyed? He loves cowboy films, he loves weepies — but he loves the fact that as a little lad, he was introduced to a new world where his own imagination could run riot.

"Some of my happiest memories were spent watching (when pocket money allowed) going to the flicks. The pictures were part of my youth. They are still a part of me. The Lost Cinemas are not lost, ironically. You only have to sit back, close your eyes and remember… "

Here are Billy's Top Five weepies . . .

The Champ – Either the original or the remake when the child cries out "CHAMP – wake up Champ!" Your heart breaks for him. Incredible acting.

Bridges of Madison County – A hauntingly beautiful tale of a secret love affair revealed after death. Superbly acted by Clint Eastwood and Meryl Streep.

Always – Such an undervalued Spielberg movie in which Richard Dreyfus returns to earth after his death as a guardian angel but finds it hard to cope watching the girl he loves being pursued by another man. He eventually has to go into her head to tell her to stop loving him. How can you do that?

Forrest Gump – Tenderly emotional. Forrest's undying love for Jenny – no matter what the cost – is superb, as is the scene where she tells Forrest the child is his and the scene where Forrest talks at her graveside, well, endless tissues needed.

The Notebook – Emotionally heart-warming, James Garner again showing what a brilliant actor he is.

YOU'VE LOST THAT LOVIN' FEELING

Tom Hanks and Robin Wright in *Forrest Gump* (1994)

Dorinda (Holly Hunter) and Pete (Richard Dreyfuss) make a toast in the 1989 film *Always*

LIVERSPOOL

Aisle of dreams

Maureen Sinclair, Director of Clapperboard UK

AT 18, I left Kirkby and moved to St Ives in Cornwall with five girlfriends and didn't return to Liverpool until 15 years later. My first job was as a part-time usherette in the local cinema The Royal, in St Ives, Cornwall.

Later, I was fortunate enough to secure a permanent job as a PA for Cinema International Corporation (an amalgamation of Paramount, Universal, MGM) in their new legal department. Back home, and with the success of Letter to Brezhnev in 1986, Liverpool City Council was inundated with enquiries from national and international film makers who were interested in using the city as a location for their films.
Looking back to my own cinema experience, when we moved to Crosby in 1986, the back of our house overlooked the Plaza Cinema, which was struggling to remain open.

I helped in the campaign to keep it open and still, to this day, organise as many events as possible there and do my best to support the local community cinema.

I've got the greatest respect for all the volunteers there. It would not remain open without their support.

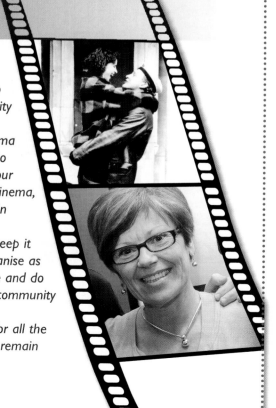

OPEN AND SHUT CASE

The Plaza opened its doors on September 2, 1939, but
was closed again that day due to the outbreak of war

"A petition to save the cinema was circulated within the local community, attracting 10,000 signatures"

COMMUNITY HEROES

Over the years, The Plaza has had to fight for survival, and once stood proudly among four other cinemas across Waterloo and Crosby.

THE Plaza cinema first opened its doors on September 2, 1939, but was almost immediately closed again that day due to regulations relating to the outbreak of war.

Fortunately, two weeks later, it was able to re-open and began a programme of films and also live variety acts from stars including Hilda Baker, Tommy Handley, Arthur Askey and Ted Ray.

There were 1000 seats in the stalls and 450 in the balcony. In 1976, it was one of the first cinemas to become a triplex, after a £100,000 scheme converted what was then called the Classic Cinema. But the cinema complex that existed then is a far cry from today.

In October 1995, the local community discovered, via a planning notice pinned to a lamp post, that the cinema site was being offered for re-development by its then owners, Apollo. ➤

➤ A major campaign was launched, through the combined efforts and determination of a group of local women who were not about to lose such a valuable community resource.

A petition to save the cinema was circulated within the local community, attracting 10,000 signatures.

This in turn was submitted to the planning department, to protest against the proposal to build offices on the site. The site subsequently went on the market.

A voluntary support shop was opened in November 1996, to raise funds from locally donated goods. This incredible display of people power was rewarded with the lease to Plaza Community Cinema – a registered charity – with an option to purchase it from the owners. The cinema re-opened on July 18, 1997, showing *Jurassic Park - The Lost World*.

In January 2000 the building was finally purchased by the charity. The move saw the Plaza diversify and attract a wider audience, despite it costing £1,000 a day to keep it running as a charity.

Offering a popular mix of blockbuster films alongside an arts screen has kept customers loyal, and in 2009 the Plaza celebrated its 70th anniversary with a special screening of the 70-year-old *Wizard of Oz*.

The film was almost destroyed after it was first shown because of poor reviews, but like the Plaza, it survived and is now an age-old classic.

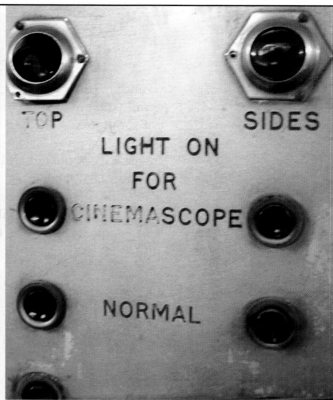

PEOPLE POWER

Top, Frank Cottrell Boyce, author and screenwriter, is an
ardent backer of this famous venue. Bottom, Liverpool actor
Ian Hart at the premiere of *A Boy Called Dad*

John 'The Duke' Wayne in a familiar Western role as Colonel Cord McNally in *Rio Lobo*

HOME ON THE RANGE

Historian John Sloan heads for the Last Chance Saloon to toast the legends of the Wild West.

MY images of the cinemas of yesteryear are as clear in my mind as the days when I visited them.

If I could put the clock back I would be happy to be stuck in that time warp. My love for the cinema developed in the late 1940s in post-war Liverpool.

Be it the picture palaces or the 'flea-pits' it was all the same to me. I suppose in some respects it was an escape from reality. A place where you could re-enact your boyhood fantasies alongside your heroes of the silver screen.

I remember with Superman's help we saved the world from the evil clutches of Atom Man. I was on top of that gas tank in *Whiteheat* with James Cagney and I helped Humphrey Bogart pull the *African Queen* through those leech-infested waters. The B-Movie Westerns were a great favourite of mine. The Durango Kid was everyone's hero. He dressed all in black and rode a white horse.

Lash LaRue could take the eye out of a rattlesnake with one crack of his whip. The favourite cowboys in these Westerns were William Boyd (Hopalong Cassidy), Charles Starrett (The Durango Kid), Jon Hall (Kit Carson), Cesar Romero (The Cisco Kid), Wild Bill Elliot, Deadwood Dick, Rocky Lane, Jonny MacBrown, Rod Cameron and John Wayne.

Then you had the singing cowboys – Gene Autry, Roy Rogers, Smiley Burnette, and the Sons of the Pioneers. The actors who played the sidekicks to these mentioned were George

GO WEST

Above: Robert Vaughn and Yul Brynner in *The Magnificent Seven*.
Right: one of Hollywood's greatest leading men, Randolph Scott

Gabby Hayes, Fuzzy Knight and Andy Devine, not forgetting Andy Clyde.

One of my favourite serials was *Nyoka the Jungle Girl*. One of the actors in this series was Clayton Moore who went on to play the Lone Ranger.

Some years later he was replaced by another actor, John Hart. Even though he wore a mask you could spot a mile away that he wasn't the original. Clayton apparently was out of contract.

You can change the actor but you can't change the voice.

Back to the flea pits and my first introduction to films was in the late forties. The so-called cinema was a glorified hut with benches for seats. It was called The Strand in Irlam Road, Bootle.

The Palace on Marsh Lane was something else. It paid you to keep your mouth shut in that place as the usherette would come round every five minutes and envelope you in a cloud of 'feit' disinfectant.

I often wondered why the ice cream had an acquired taste. During the interval the Pearl and Dean adverts would flash onto the screen. They would depict a glamorous young lady selling refreshments.

A far cry from what we were confronted with, our hostess looked as if she had gone ten rounds at the Liverpool Stadium.

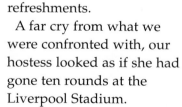

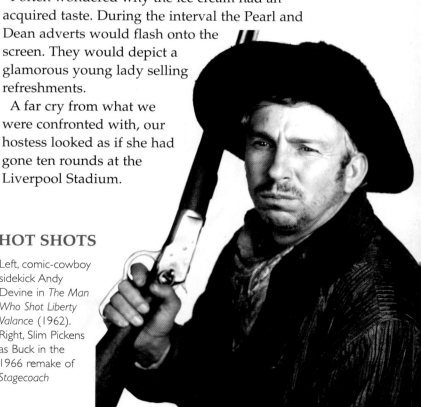

HOT SHOTS

Left, comic-cowboy sidekick Andy Devine in *The Man Who Shot Liberty Valance* (1962). Right, Slim Pickens as Buck in the 1966 remake of *Stagecoach*

FILMS IN THE KEY OF LIFE

Phil Key, journalist and former arts editor for the Liverpool Daily Post, recalls a close encounter with a Titan of the movie world.

ACCESS ALL AREAS

Phil Key joins the Odeon queue to watch *Spiceworld* in 1997

THERE is always a welcoming place in any strange city as I discovered when I first arrived in Liverpool in 1968. It was the cinema.

When you are alone there is something comforting about sitting in the dark watching familiar faces on the screen and feeling part of a crowd.

Although even then cinemas were closing I found plenty still operating in the city centre and the suburbs and all friendly places to visit.

I remember vividly watching Walt Disney's *Jungle Book* at the Albany, Maghull, and *The Wizard of Oz* at the Phoenix in Wallasey, both cinemas built in the 1950s but with welcoming aspects.

Then there was the glorious Abbey Cinerama in Wavertree where I watched *2001* and was totally amazed by the imagination of its director Stanley Kubrick, the scenes in space totally convincing on the enormous screen, rather less so on the video version I was to buy later.

Most of my film-going was to be done in the city centre, however, where there were numerous delights, even a cartoon cinema for a while in the old Tatler in Church Street which had been renamed the Classic Cartoon Cinema, very handy for shoppers wanting a short break from consumerism.

I enjoyed foreign films but found only one commercial cinema showing them and that was the Jacey Cinema in Clayton Square where I saw Czech director Milos Forman's *The Fireman's Ball*. Unfortunately the cinema tended to concentrate on sexy movies so the support movie was a nudist film.

The cinema closed in 1972 – the last film was *The Subject is Sex* – and strangely reopened as a church, The Shrine of the Blessed Sacrament.

One of the newest cinemas was the Studio 1, 2 and 3 in Brownlow Hill, built in 1985, which also went on the sex route later. Before then, I had gone to see director Mel Brooks's *Silent Movie* at a matinee and found myself the only customer. They do say comedies need a big audience but I laughed like an idiot all the way through that film.

It was at the ABC Forum, if memory serves, that I had my creepiest film-going experience. The film was *The Exorcist* and there had been reports of people fainting at screenings. Lined up at the back of the cinema were St John's Ambulance personnel which made me even more nervous. I did not faint but several people left before the end, ashen-faced.

For many years I was film critic of the Liverpool Daily Post and had the privilege of watching films in VIP comfort at a number of Liverpool cinemas. My favourite was the Odeon in London Road, largely thanks to the manager at the time, George Cranfield, one of

An epic drama of adventure and exploration

2001: a space odyssey

WILLIAM PETER BLATTY'S

THE EXORCIST

Directed by WILLIAM FRIEDKIN

"I enjoyed being chased down London Road by St Trinian's girls and faced a gorgeous female model in boxing gloves to promote a Rocky film"

THAT'S ENTERTAINMENT

The Odeon, London Road, in 1975. Below, The Tatler on Church Street, in 1963 – a city centre refuge from the 'real' world

the old school managers, strict but always jolly good company at the end of a showing where he would entertain in his room with food and drink.

He also loved the occasional publicity drive and I enjoyed being chased down London Road by some St Trinian's girls and faced by a gorgeous female model in boxing gloves to promote a Rocky film.

There were also visits by big film names. At the ABC Forum I upset special effects master Ray Harryhausen, promoting his *Clash of the Titans* in 1981. Perhaps fuelled by too much hospitality, I did wonder why his special effects creatures never looked real. I won't report his reply except to say that he was not pleased . . .

JAWS OPENER

Queues in Lime Street wait to snap up a ticket for the monster hit Jaws in 1975 – a scene you seldom see these days as film-goers have multiscreen options . . .

A TECHNICOLOUR TREAT

When all you had at home was a black and white telly, a trip to the cinema was a magical experience, says Fred Lawless, playwriter and screenwriter.

WALKING into a picture house for the first time I was immediately struck by the sheer size of the screen and the vivid colours. When all you had at home (if you were lucky) was a small, grainy black and white telly, it was little wonder that small kids would gawp at that screen open-mouthed in amazement.

My first introduction to cinema was the cartoon films that the Tatler on Church Street and the Jacey in Clayton Square would churn out daily.

The films were on a loop so you'd often hear parents announcing: "This is where we came in", which was the cue for lots of arguing from kids trying to convince their mums and dads they hadn't seen this one yet – no kid was EVER in a hurry to leave.

Sadly, both those picture houses eventually closed, but by then I'd outgrown cartoons and was now ready for a proper movie.

The first feature film I saw in a picture house was Disney's *In Search of The Castaways*, starring a teenage Hayley Mills at the Futurist on Lime Street.

It was a very special moment for me and as an adult I've resisted watching the film again on DVD as I know it won't be the same magical experience it was the first time.

I don't want my wonderful childhood memory of the occasion to be tarnished.

But it wasn't just the feature film that made going to the pictures

special, it was the whole occasion. The smell of popcorn, the added attraction of the unknown 'B' movie that would precede the main feature, the trailers for forthcoming movies that would whet our appetites for a future visit.

The massive leap TV technology has taken means no child will ever walk into a cinema and be enthralled at what they see in the same way I and millions of others were.

Nowadays kids have libraries of DVD films in their bedrooms and every night can watch a film if they choose. A good thing? In some ways maybe, but the 'specialness' of the occasion has gone.

Walking into those beautiful art deco buildings, being escorted to your seat by torchlight, watching eerie wisps of cigarette smoke slowly glide across the screen, and hearing the occasional sensual moan from the lovers on the back seat.

Meanwhile, those majestic buildings have been demolished or converted to supermarkets and bingo halls. Hollywood has survived and cinema has also lived on, but only by way of the multiplex cinemas sited in out of town retail parks.

They still give that big screen experience, but the magic of the local and city centre picture houses has gone.

In Liverpool we still cling valiantly to a couple that have survived, the Woolton Picture House in particular is very close to my heart and I urge everyone to support this wonderful cinema whenever they can.

Trevor Horn, a record producer, once sang that "Video Killed The Radio Star" . . . some would argue that its worse crime was killing Picture Houses. He later paid tribute to Ealing Studios.

Things do go full circle.

Liverpool News Theatre in Clayton Square, pictured in 1947

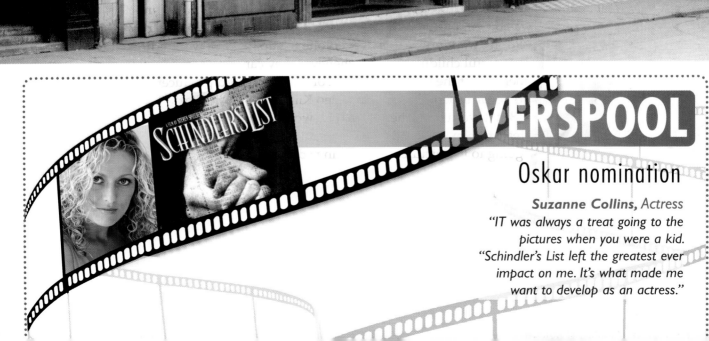

LIVERSPOOL

Oskar nomination

Suzanne Collins, *Actress*
"IT was always a treat going to the pictures when you were a kid. "Schindler's List left the greatest ever impact on me. It's what made me want to develop as an actress."

A WARTIME SURVIVOR

NEW SPIN

Since opening in 1927, Woolton Picture House has survived WW2 bombing raids, a fire and repeated threats of closure, but remains a much-loved part of the community

A jewel in the cultural life of South Liverpool, Woolton Picture House remains Liverpool's oldest surviving independent single screen cinema.

WOOLTON Picture House first opened between December 1927 and February 1928, although the cinema celebrates its opening on December 26.

The building was designed by the architect A G Pritchard, who designed many of Merseyside's cinemas, including The Plaza at Crosby.

Originally it had a capacity of 800 seats, but this was reduced when the screen was brought forward to accommodate large loud speakers behind it.

This proved to be a shrewd move with the huge popularity of talking pictures.

The cinema managed to survive the bombing raids in WW2, broadcasting regular bulletins through the Pathé News Reel.

Disaster struck in September 1958, when a fire nearly destroyed the auditorium. The cinema was forced to close for three months, re-opening in December.

The cinema continued to remain open, under changing ownership, always managing to keep up with technological advances while preserving its Art Deco interior, until closure was threatened in the 1990s.

Luckily, in 1992, and to the great relief of the local community, its ownership changed hands to David Wood, grandson of John F Wood, the local cinema pioneer who had opened Liverpool's first purpose built cinema, the Bedford, in 1907, and who was responsible for the Abbey Cinerama.

The future appeared brightly technicoloured, until the death of David Swindell, chief projectionist for 40 years, followed swiftly by the death of owner David Wood.

Closure followed in 2006, but this much-loved cinema was not going to be given up without a fight.

A campaign was launched, with a number of fundraising events being staged – one of which saw the reforming of The Quarrymen.

The campaign attracted the support of an anonymous consortium of local businessmen, which enabled the cinema to open its doors again.

A VISION FOR THE FUTURE

Joan Burnett, Visitor Services Manager at FACT (Foundation for Art and Creative Technology), on the renaissance of cinema.

"Technology, innovation and a close connection to the local community will keep cinema alive and kicking"

THE cinemas that helped to make my childhood extra special have long gone – The Phoenix and the Unit Four in Wallasey are just ghosts in a modern streetscape – but on Merseyside, we are now lucky enough to have the best cinema provision we've had for years with even more opportunities on the horizon. The renaissance of cinema may seem unexpected, but it's been no surprise to me.

Talking to audiences at my beloved FACT, I know there's a hunger out there for every kind of cinema. Venues like the Odeon and FACT have had to make huge investment to bring their customers 3D and HD technology and there's a growing awareness that audiences want a wider variety of film.

FACT's funky Box cinema with its sofa-style seating makes an intimate space for the way out and wonderful.

It's often a stop-off for proud Scousers showing visitors to Liverpool the best it has to offer, along with Epstein's Dickie Lewis statue and the Philharmonic Gents!

Independent voices are being heard too, with film clubs happening in café venues courtesy of local film activists and the Small Cinema which pops up wherever it can find a home.

Urban Strawberry Lunch have their

marvellous open-air film programme at St Luke's (the 'Bombed-Out Church') and the Wirral International Film Festival gives new film a boost with its open submissions policy.

Abandon Normal Devices will return to Liverpool in 2011 bringing its bold approach, screening film in both conventional and outlandish settings and trailing the national press in its wake.

Other local festivals bring us a marvellous diversity of film: the Arabic Arts and Liverpool Irish Festival screenings, films from Da Da Fest and the Plaza's recent OPEN festival, bringing LGBT film to local audiences in North Liverpool.

Venues like St George's Hall are getting in on the act with large one-off events and hundreds of people have turned out to see films like *Of Time and the City* and *On The Waterfront* screened outdoors at Kings Dock.

Merseyside's passion for film is unabated: we love to watch films and be seen in them – Liverpool is the second most filmed city in England after London after all. Young people are proving the lifeblood of new cinema, with vibrant youth groups at The Plaza, Freehand at FACT and the Clapperboard crew all making new work using digital technology.

This new brand of cinema brings the process of film-making right to our doorstep and points to the future – technology, innovation and a close connection to the local community will keep cinema alive and kicking.

SPEX APPEAL

Clockwise from left: 3D action at Liverpool ONE Odeon; FACT's 'Box' cinema; the spectacular setting for open-air film screenings at St Luke's Church

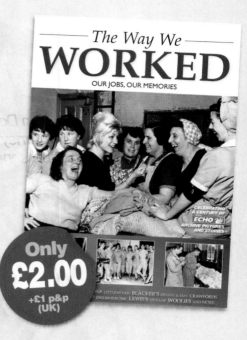

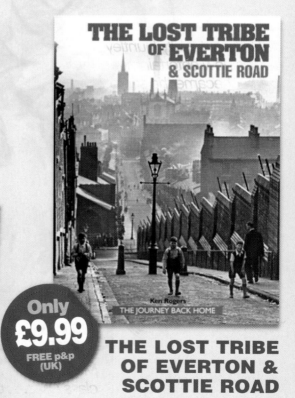

"Are yer dancin'?" "Are yer askin'?"

Send us your stories and you could have a starring role in our next archive special...

THERE was a time when gliding and spinning across the dance floor, under glitter balls and subtle lighting in a myriad of famous venues, was THE number one entertainment activity for every adult on Merseyside.

Did you visit places like the Grafton, Locarno, Orrell Park Ballroom, the Rialto, Peppers on Aubrey Street, Blair Hall on Walton Road, or Reece's in the city centre?

Have you got vivid memories of giant venues like the Tower Ballroom in New Brighton, and St George's Hall, or have you got personal dance tales about smaller district venues that have long since drifted out of our psyche? Have you ever been knocked back on the dance floor after asking: "Are yer dancin'?"

Or were you one of those men with two left feet who stood on the fringe of the floor for hours, terrified to cross the line into that seething mass of swaying and rhythmic inter-action?

We want to hear from you as we prepare a fascinating magazine that will bring back some fantastic memories of the real-life 'Strictly Come Dancing' era. Send your stories and pictures to: Peter Grant, Liverpool Daily Post & Echo, Old Hall Street, Liverpool L69 3EB, or email petergrant@liverpoolecho.co.uk

THE LIGHTS GO UP

And now, those two words all cinema-goers hate . . . The End.

THIS production is a classic and will run and run. But now we must grab our coats and roll the final credits – where the thousands who worked on the films we watch get their name check.

In the old days, the staccato machine-gun rattle of seats heralded the end of the film – along with the National Anthem. Long gone but not forgotten. Leaving the warm cinema for the outside cold is always the saddest part.

And, yet, you know you can always go again tomorrow and the next day and the day after. The lost cinemas are just that – 'lost' in a memory. No special effects will bring them back, but their physical presence and memories that they created linger on.

Some cinemas are no more – The Mayfair in Aigburth Road is now a Home Bargains store; the Abbey Cinerama is past its shelf date and now a Morrisons supermarket; the Lime Street Scala is a nightclub. The Gaumont in Anfield is a community arts centre. The Cameo Cinema in Wavertree, which made headlines in the 50s for all the wrong reasons when it was the subject of a real murder story, is now an apartment block.

Some cinemas have bravely fought off the march of time and remain picture palaces to this very day where past meets present.

You've read about them here – now go back and support them.

The magic of the movies will always be with us. From Walt Disney to Harry Potter; from Sherlock Holmes to Shrek. We all love it.

The last picture show? Happily, there's no such thing . . .

The End